Malbork

Mieczysław Haftka
Mariusz Mierzwiński

Malbork

Castle of the Teutonic Order

© RV Reise- und Verkehrsverlag GmbH
Berlin · Gütersloh · Leipzig · München · Potsdam · Stuttgart 1992

Photo on front cover: Malbork on the Nogat, Photo Press
Cartography: RV Reise- und Verkehrsverlag GmbH, Berlin · Gütersloh · Leipzig · München · Potsdam · Stuttgart 1992
Illustrations: Mariusz Mierzwiński, Malbork: page 2, 8, 10, 12/13, 15, 18, 20, 21, 23, 24/25, 26, 29, 30, 31, 32, 34, 36/37, 38, 39, 40, 41, 42, 46, 47, 48, 50, 51, 52/53, 54, 56, 57, 58, 60, 62, 64/65, 66, 67, 68, 71, 72/73, 74, 75, 77, 78, 81, 82/83, 84, 85, 86, 88/8, 91, 92/93, 94/95; Photo Press, Taufkirchen/München: page 6/7, 17, 44/45, 63.

Authors: Mieczysław Haftka, Sopot; Mariusz Mierzwiński, Malbork
English Translation: Eliza Lewandowska, Warsaw
Idea and series conception: Prisma Verlag GmbH, Munich
Edited and coordination by: Prisma Verlag GmbH, Munich with the assistance of GeoCenter, Warsaw
Cover layout: Prisma Verlag GmbH, Munich

Typesetting: Buchmacher Bär, Freising
Reproduction: Master Fotolito, Milano
Printing and finish: Mohndruck Graphische Betriebe GmbH, Gütersloh

Printed in Germany
ISBN: 3-575-22077-8

Contents

Above: The High Castle from the north-east.
Page 2: The western cloister in the High Castle.
Page 6/7: Malbork on the Nogat. Castle of the Teutonic Order.

8

Introduction

The establishment of the medieval defence complex of Malbork, made up of a triple-structured castle and the fortified town, was linked up with the activity of the Order of the Hospital of Our Lady of the German House, known as the Ordo Teutonicorum, the Teutonic Order. The huge, over 20-hectare-large (about 50-acre) stronghold has its significant place in the history of Europe and even in its most recent history. Here, within the walls of the castle-monastery and town as hardly anywhere else, the fragments of Polish and German history as well as the tragic fate of the Prussians, Lithuanians and Samogitians closely converge. Over a span of seven ages history also marked this place out for a meeting place of the Czech, Swedish, French and Russian forces.

Almost every era and every war episode left a trace of itself in Malbork's historical walls as well as in its topography. Most visible are the traces of the Second World War, which had such tragic effects on this historical complex. The large rebuilt parts of the walls, distinguished by their brighter shade of brick, are evidence of the great amount of conservation work that had to be carried out in order to restore the invaluable monument of medieval fortification art after its destruction in March 1945. At the moment reconstruction is nearing its end. However, other threats that are no smaller have appeared: the effects of industrialization.

We present this book on Malbork in the faith that it will encourage the reader to visit the castle. We are fully aware that even the best description of a work of art cannot replace the joy of direct contact with it.

Mariusz Mierzwiński
Director of the Castle-Museum

Mieczysław Haftka
Vice-director of the Castle-Museum

9

Hermann von Salza (1209-1239). Engraving by Ch. Hartknoch, 1684.

The Teutonic Order
until 1225

Orders of knighthood rose in the atmosphere of the crusades. The concept of liberating the Holy Land from Muslim oppression, put forward by Pope Urban II in 1095, was widely reflected in Christian Europe. It was carried out during the first crusade. It turned out, however, that it was easier to conquer these lands than to maintain the Kingdom of Jerusalem in Palestine. From the beginning of its existence the young Christian state met with serious difficulties in defending its borders and its administrative body, and most of all it had difficulties in ensuring protection and basic living standards for the pilgrims massively coming to the Holy Sepulchre. In this difficult situation the voluntary knighthood and Samaritan service came into being. It took on organized forms when the volunteers acting in accordance with the ideal of helping one's neighbours established charity corporations. From these the following orders of knighthood were formed within the 12th century: the Hospitalers, the Templars and the Teutonic Knights. While the individual actions and national ambitions of these groups may arouse controversy, the motives of the establishment of the Order of the Hospital of Our Lady of the German House in Jerusalem do not give rise to any doubts. From the German hospital brotherhood, operating in Jerusalem from 1128 onwards, the Teutonic Order developed in 1190. It gathered in its ranks knights of German origin. Apart from the tasks officially announced and ensuing from the adopted rule (bringing help to pilgrims, mainly from Germany, and defending the Holy Land), it had to ensure stable support and to represent the interests of the empire on the Levantine lands.

With time, as land endowments became more frequent in Europe and Asia, non-German origin was not compulsory. However, knowledge of the German language was required, yet this rule was also abandoned in the course of time. For the Lotharingian section for example the rule was translated into French. The Order had an international character, but the great majority of its members was of German origin.

Life in the orders was based on the rule, a collection of regulations that were obligatory for all members of an order. The first version of the rule of the Teutonic Order was approved by

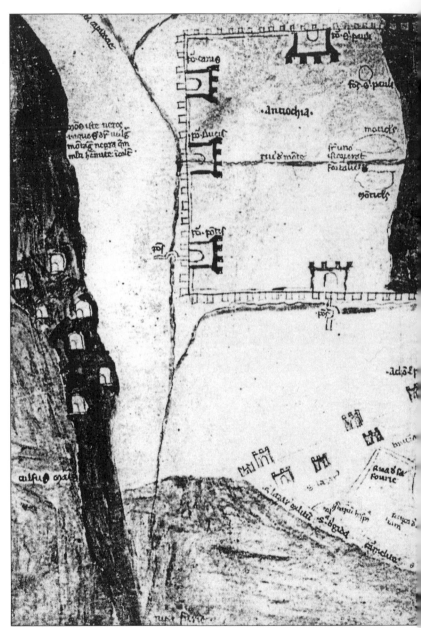

City map of Akkon. Pencil drawing from the early 14th century.

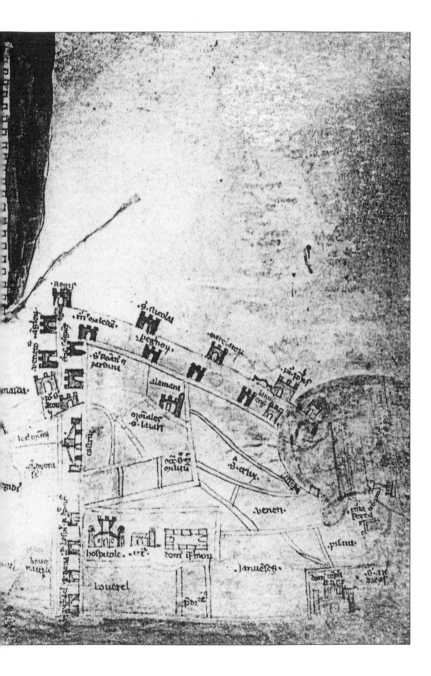

13

Pope Innocent III in 1199 and was a compilation of statutes of the Templars and the Hospitalers.

With time, orders of knighthood were relieved from the control of the local church as well as of secular authority and were directly subordinated to the Roman curia and thus constituted separate »states within a state«. This was, as it turned out, dangerous for the fate of the Kingdom of Jerusalem and also tragic for the Order on the territory of Transylvania (Hungary). On the other hand, the protection of the Holy See to a large extent brought about the creation of the Order's state in Prussia.

The Teutonic Order was governed by autonomous authority – the General Chapter, headed by the Grand Master, appointed for a life time. The General Chapter consisted of members of the main house and the domestic masters, who governed the individual provinces of the Order. The supreme executive authority was vested in the Grand Master. The significance of the General Chapter diminished when the main house of the Order was moved from Venice to Malbork in favour of a council appointed by the Grand Master. It comprised the highest five dignitaries (the Grand Commander – deputy of the Grand Master, the Grand Marshal, the Grand Hospitaler, the Grand Cloak Bearer, the Grand Treasurer) and two Commanders. From the 14th century they were the actual rulers of the Order.

The basic family of the Order was formed by a monastery consisting of at least twelve knight-brothers, six clergy members and the Commander. However, in Prussia these proportions were not always kept. Sometimes monasteries numbered fifty and more knight-brothers. The monastery was governed by the Commander, who also had military, administrative and judicial authority within the organizational unit. This unit was called »komturia« and was subordinated to him. The brothers, apart from caring for the poor and sick, also took on the duty of fighting the unfaithful. This was one of the basic tasks that the rule defined. In accordance with its statutes, monks were divided into knights, chaplains, menial brothers and half-brothers. The first two groups took vows. The brother-knights came from the higher feudal strata and when being accepted to the Order had to give evidence of nobility. All distinctions in the Order were reserved for this group only. It was they who in fact made the decisions and determined the policy of the Order.

Chaplains were selected from clergymen who were ordained and their acceptance to the monastery was not determined by social origin.

Banner of the Order's Grand Master.

To the third, the most numerous group – that of menial brothers, all secular brothers were admitted who did not have sufficient qualifications to be admitted to the group, because in its structure class division had clearly been visible from the beginning. The Order did not make high demands on newcomers. It was enough to know the basic prayers within a half-year novitiate. The rule preferred a brother-knight to an ascetic monk.

A knight had to be always ready to fight. Statutes of the orders and the military regulations defined the place and duties of a knight during war and peace. In case of a misdemeanor all sorts of punishments were applied, including expulsion from the order.

Chaplains were engaged in ministration and were also in charge of a chancellery because they were educated persons.

The lowest offices which had to do with economic and military affairs were held by the menial brothers under the supervision of the brother-knights.

The rule, at the beginning established for a small group only, became impractical in many clauses as the Order expanded. This became clearly visible during the rule of Grand Master Hermann von Salza (1209-1239).

The spirit of enterprise of the Teutonic Knights was impressive. In the thirteenth century they obtained a series of endowments, mainly in Germany, Italy and other European countries as well as in Asia.

From the very beginning of its existence the Teutonic Order was characterized by an active attitude, political cunning, the ability of transferring any innovations to their own territory but also by various types of misuses.

Three times the Order participated in the organization of a church state. The first time it formed part of the crusades in Palestine. Later it acted already independently in Transylvania and finally in Prussia. The third attempt was fully successful. However, it was preceded by the long diplomatic campaign carefully prepared by Hermann von Salza.

The failures in Palestine and Hungary made the Order turn its attention to the Baltic territories inhabited by pagan tribes: Prussians, Lithuanians, Latvians, Samogitians and Finns, Estonians and Livonians.

Hermann von Salza knew much about Europe's political situation of those days. In his view, the Baltic and Finnish countries were a much more convenient territory for German colonization than Palestine, which was constantly endangered by the growing power of the Arabs. It is most probably on the grounds of his inspiration that Frederick II, Emperor of Rome, proclaimed a manifesto in which he summoned the pagan nations of this part of Europe to adopt Christianity. In the understanding of those times such an appeal was the starting point for organizing crusades. Arousing the interest of the pope as well as of the emperor, Hermann von Salza presumably intended to derive benefit for the Order from this undertaking. No doubt he was counting on the elimination of earlier missions, mainly Cistercian, which had been working on the territory of Latvia from the 2nd

Statue of Grand Master Winrich von Kniprode.

half of the 12th century and in Prussia from the beginning of the 13th century. In the near future he showed that he was an unusually consistent politician. By attaining the endowment of the district of Chelmno from Prince Konrad Mazowiecki (in 1225) and linking his order with the Order of the Knights of the Sword (in 1237), he created the real foundations of the future Teutonic state in Prussia.

Battle between Prussians and Teutonic Knights. Illustration on a pillar in the refectory of the former infirmary, 14th century.

The Prussians,
Poland's Neighbours

Apart from Latvians, Lithuanians and Samogitians, the Baltic tribes also included Prussians who inhabited the area between the lower Vistula and Niemen Rivers. In the 13th century the Polish principalities bordered with them in the south and the west.

The Prussians emerged as a separate ethnic group at the turn of antiquity to the early Middle Ages. In spite of many common concepts and archaic forms, their language differed from the language - of the neighbouring Lithuanians, Latvians and Samogitians. The extremely long time of neighbourhood with the Slavs also had its influence on the language in the form of many borrowed words.

In the middle of the 9th century the name »Prussians« was first used by an anonymous chronicler from the Benedictine abbey in Fulda, called the Bavarian Geographer. From that time on the name remained but its etymology has not yet been fully explained. Most probably it comes from the occupation that is characteristic of Prussians, namely horse breeding, because in the language of the Kashubians, the western neighbours of Prussia, the word »prus« designates a stallion.

At the beginning of the 13th century the area of Prussia encompassed about 42,000 sq km and according to estimations was inhabited by about 137,000 people. Their religion was limited to the cult of natural forces; they worshipped the sun, the moon, the stars, lightnings as well as animals. Cults were performed in »holy« groves, fields and waters. According to the beliefs of the Prussians, all nature was marked with a divine element. In spiritual life great significance was given to the cult of the dead, who were burnt at the stake.

At the beginning of the 13th century Prussia was divided into 10 large territories (Pomezania, Pogczania, Warmia, Natangia, Sambia, Nadrowia, Skalowia, Sudowia, Galindia and Barcja). In written sources they were described as »terra« – land. In the 14th century the most complete catalogue of these was written down by the chronicler Piotr Dusburg with the addition of the district of Chełmno, which was not inhabited by Prussians. Each district comprised several »terrul« or »territoria« – small lands. These in turn were divided into the smallest units called »lauks«. Their

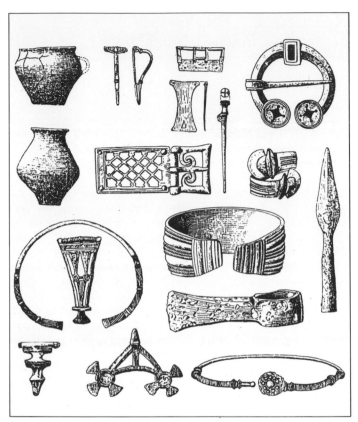

Historical items of the Baltic culture.

number and size varied, most probably depending on the degree of economic development. It is also difficult to discern any consistent scheme in the layout of strongholds.

As a rule, free people lived in one-manor settlements loosely scattered over the »lauks«, around which the settlers cultivated as much land as they needed. The land was the property of the settler who had the right of succession.

For a long time the social system of Prussia was a continuation of the tribal structure. At the turn of antiquity to the early Middle Ages a transition to the class system and consequently, during the 7th-10th century, to the establishment of three social strata began: the magnates, the free people and the slaves. An expression of the

Picture of a Prussian woman with her jewellery; after Romuald Odoj.

new socio-economic structure was the formation of war democracy as its political organization. In consequence, this would gradually lead to the formation of the tribal system with the prince as the head. This, however, did not take place in Prussia because the conservative factor that limited the powers and position of the chiefs (of strongholds) was the rally. At these rallies the free people of the territorial unit made the most important decisions concerning its community. The other factor that hampered the inheritance of power was the case law. Most of all it limited the possibilities of becoming more wealthy within a family by way of inheritance after death. The funeral customs, noted down by the Anglo-Saxon seafarer Wulfstan at the end of the 9th century and accompanied by funeral banquets lasting for many days, absorbed the wealth of the deceased. The remaining movable property was held ready as awards for the victors of the chase organized on this occasion. Such a customary-legal state lasted until the 14th century, when it was noted by Dusburg. The system of war democracy had two most important factors: the rally as the most significant authority during peace and the elected chief for the time of war – are characteristic elements of the political life in Prussia in the 12th and 13th century. With time it underwent further transformation. Under the pressure of the magnates, an additional rally was established, called the war rally. This provided the possibility of increasing the number of expeditions, which above all brought wealth to the higher strata. This is linked with the intensification of the Prussian expansion, especially the plundering invasions on Mazovia and Gdansk Pomerania from the middle of the 12th century.

On the other hand, the significance of the chiefs elected by the rally increased with the intensification of external danger. In times of war they obtained considerable power. They were entitled to collect the necessary fees, to fortify the country and gather the people for defence. Finally, they decided on the defensive as well as on the offensive tactics. An additional element was the multifarious and multiform landscape of Prussia with its countless lakes, marshland, rivers and large woodlands. The dense network of strongholds, wire entanglements, ramparts combined with the natural defence conditions created a cohesive defence system which was difficult to conquer. For these reasons most expeditions into Prussia's interior were organized in winter.

From the second half of the 12th century the feudalization processes were accelerated and the plundering invasions of Prussia into neighbouring lands increased. These were followed by migrations of their people.

Broken up into districts, Poland was unable to check the Prussians. For the Polish princes the Prussian problem did not begin at the end of the 12th century. Prussia had been within the centre of interest of Poland since the time of Bolesław Chrobry. An expression of the expansive policy of the early-Piast monarchy

Page from the German-Prussian dictionary, 16th century.

was the mission of Saint Adalbert in 997 as well as further Christianization campaigns and expeditions of Polish kings and princes. Towards the end of the 12th and at the beginning of the 13th century attempts were made to organize a border »guard«, at first consisting of the knights from Poland's interior, then of the orders of knighthood.

From the beginning of the 13th century (1206) a mission of Polish Cistercians headed by Bishop Chrystian began its work in the areas neighbouring on the district of Chelmno and Pomerania,

Frieze at a fire-place: Battle between Teutonic Knights and Prussians.

i.e. Pomezania and Pogezania. Its strength was the generally proclaimed concept of Christianization and crusades. The world's attention was drawn to the last enclaves of paganism in Europe, first on the Polabian Slavs, then on the Baltic peoples.

During this time there was a growing tension at the Mozovian-Prussian border caused by the pressure of the crusaders, bound by the pope at the council of 1215 to defend Christians against the pagans in the Baltic countries. Thus the mission in Prussia became an international problem, and in 1217 Bishop Chrystian obtained from Pope Honorius III the official leadership of the missions and crusades in Prussia. This led to further aggravation of the

Mazovian-Prussian relations. In 1220 the Prussians, collaborating with the Ruthenian Prince Daniel, defeated the forces of Konrad Mazowiecki. In subsequent years there were mutual retaliatory expeditions, as a result of which the Prussians destroyed Płock and the monastery of the Cistercians in Oliwa.

Page from the »Wiesenbuch« of the city of Elbląg, 1421.

The Teutonic Order
in Prussia

The complicated Prussian question terminated Polish political influence in this country, and for Konrad I Mazowiecki, the most interested of the district princes, it made the designed participation in the fight for the Cracow throne more difficult.

It is not known who exactly suggested to Konrad I to bring in the Teutonic Order. The first negotiations of interested parties are mentioned in the declaration of Emperor Frederick II for the Order from 1226. According to this document, Konrad Mazowiecki promised to give the district of Chełmno back to the Order and in addition provided it with another district at the border in return for the Order's conquest of Prussia.

Along with Konrad's proposal emerged the opportunity of realizing the endeavours of the Order to build a state. Hermann von Salza carefully prepared his plan. He turned to the emperor to approve the land endowments from Prince Konrad. In 1226 Frederick II approved the grant and conferred the title to all the pagan lands that the Prussians were to conquer in Prussia. At the same time he conferred to the Order the same rights and privileges that the Reich princes had. This act became the »corner stone« for the organization of the Order's future state in Prussia. Its contents, however, was in contradiction to the papal bans of 1216 and 1220, which forbade the order to accept any benefices from secular parties. It was also in conflict with the Polish understanding of the character of the land endowments. As the donor, Prince Konrad did not resign from the right of his suzerainty. This is clearly confirmed by the feudal privilege of Konrad for the Order from 1228. One statement runs that handing over to foreign hands the district of Chełmno, which constituted a part of the heritage of the whole Piast dynasty, requires the consent of all the Polish princes. As is known, no such consent was ever given.

The legal concepts adopted in Poland had a somewhat different meaning in the countries of Western Europe, where an endowment could be equivalent to the renunciation of the suzerainty title. Hermann von Salza understood this difference and quickly arranged for an imperial privilege. Thus the Order, which according to Konrad's plans was to create conditions for the political expansion in Prussia, in fact began organizing a sovereign state. Unaware of the danger, Konrad as well as other bishops supported the actions of the Order in Prussia in the beginning.

The Teutonic crusade in Prussia began in 1231 when the first domestic master, Hermann von Balk, »crossed« the Vistula and rebuilt the stronghold around which the town of Toruń grew in a short time. In the next year the Order conquered the chief stronghold of the Chełmno district – Chełmno. Towards the end of 1234 the first expedition into Prussia was organized under participation of the German and Polish knights. The stronghold of Kwidzyń was taken as well as the Pomezans' Prussian forces at Dzierzgoń River.

The conquest of Prussia began with the taking of lands situated along the right bank of Vistula River all the way up to the Baltic. Then the crusaders set out for the east, along the way setting up new wooden-earth watch towers in place of the burnt and destroyed Prussian strongholds. With time these were in many cases rebuilt into stone and brick defence castles. The tactics were simple and were supported by iron discipline. The conquest was made along the main water routes. The stronghold was taken, then rebuilt, with the crusaders settling in it. Its task was to defend the conquered territory, its roads and passes, as well as to maintain the watch tower until the next crusade. In this manner, a dense network of fortifications of the Order gradually covered the taken Prussian lands.

In the years 1236-1238 the strong resistance of the Pogazans was subdued near Lake Drużno, and a watch tower was established in Elblag (1237) and Dzierzgoń (1238). Then the Warmians, Natangians and Barts were conquered and small strongholds were established in Bartoszyce, Balda and Reszel. Nearly simultaneously, crusades set out in the direction of the wealthiest district of Prussia – Sambia. The conquest of the Prussian lands lasted until 1283, interrupted by desperate risings of the Prussian population. The lack of central headquarters and of the modern tactics of the Teutonic forces determined the ultimate defeat of the Prussians.

At the time of these military actions, Hermann von Salza launched an intensive diplomatic campaign, aiming at eliminating competitive missions from the Prussian territories. As a result of his consistent efforts, Pope Gregory IX issued a bull in 1234, on behalf of which the missionary Prussian bishop Chrystian, held in captivity by the Prussians in the years 1233-1239, lost the function of a papal deputy in this country. In fact, the bull constituted an autonomous state of the Order and announced the necessity of creating a church organization that would be different from that visualized by Chrystian. In 1236 the papal legate William of Modena re-

Feudal privilege, issued by Pope Innocent IV, 1243.

ceived the instruction to divide Prussia into three dioceses. The release of Bishop Chrystian from captivity stopped the realization of these plans for a short time. However, the rivalry was won by the Teutonic Knights because as early as in 1243, while Chrystian was still alive, the borders were marked out for the new dioceses Chełmińska, Pomezańska, Warmińska and Sambijska.

Along with the progressing conquest the new administrative division was begun. As a rule, the newly organized network of »komturias« and »komornictwos« referred to earlier divisions. Within the district of Aliem, whose principal stronghold was presumably situated in Sztum, the Teutonic Knights established a »komturia« in Zantyr. This solution was determined by organizational, economic and military aspects. Zantyr, located at the fork of the Vistula and Nogat Rivers, had for a long time been a strong and well organized Pomeranian castellan stronghold. From 1230 it was the seat of the centre of Bishop Chrystian's Prussian mission, with a church that was destroyed during the Thirteen Years' War. During Chrystian's captivity the stronghold was taken by the Teutonic Knights. In the years 1280-1281 the convent left the stronghold in

Drawing of a tombstone-plate of von Liebenstein, late 14th cent.

30

Tympanum at the main gate of the »kumtur«-castle in Birgelau.

Zantyr and settled in the newly built castle in Malbork, thus marking the beginning of the »komturia« of Malbork.

The expansion of the Order to lands that were originally Polish gave rise to a long-lasting conflict. Attempts to regain the lost lands ended in failure for both the militant Władysław Łokietek and for Kazimierz the Great, who opted for diplomatic solutions. The great war Poland waged with the Order brought no decisive solutions either, although the defeat at Grunwald extremely disturbed the power of the Teutonic Knights. The return of the conquered lands happened right after the Thirteen Years' War, after the Peace of Toruń in 1466.

In 1525 the last Grand Master, residing in Królewiec, dissolved the Order and adopted the Protestant faith. The secularization of the Teutonic state followed, and a secular principality was established as fief of the Polish Crown.

The High Castle in winter.

The Beginnings of the Construction of the Castle and Town

Historical sources mentioned Malbork rather late. The oldest reference to it dates back to 1280. The name »Sanctemarienburch«, written down in the charter of the town from 1286, is most often derived from the order's patroness – Saint Mary.

However, there are some circumstances that link the name of Malbork with an earlier centre of the worship of Saint Mary. It is identified on the one hand with the place in which at present stands the church of Saint George, and on the other hand with the lost medieval picture of Our Lady.

Most probably in 1280, the Order's convent moved from Zantyr to Malbork. The last Commander in Zantyr and the first in Malbork was Henry von Wildenau.

It can be supposed that before the »komturia« was transferred, a provisional convent house was prepared in Malbork. It is not clear when exactly the construction work began. The preliminary stage of work was most probably very brief (1278-1280) because there is no mention of the new castle in Dusburg's chronicle, which describes the last invasion of the Samogitians into the district of Chelmno and Pomezania in 1277.

The castle and town of Malbork were situated in a place characteristic of defence structures. The fortification complex of Malbork was raised at the northern edge of a narrow, long and at the same time high peninsula. From the west and partly from the north access was made difficult by Nogat River and from the east by the wide marshy valley. The most favourable access was from the south. From this side the first fortifications were most probably built, originally of wood and earth, shortly after changed into solid brick walls.

The topography of the area determined the layout of the fortification complex. This concerns the town in particular, and in part also the High Castle and the Middle Castle. The whole was established along a high bank of Nogat River, on a high peninsula visibly standing out against the surrounding marshland and water. This explains above all the elongated shape of the town, which did not have the classic market square. Its function was fulfilled by the main street, in which the parish church of Saint John and the town hall stood.

The »Gdanisko« Tower in the High Castle.

Originally the town was much narrower, and later, in 1388, the old 13th-century suburbs were incorporated into its limits. These suburbs were inhabited by an international community without a self-government and were directly subordinated to the jurisdiction of the Commander. On this occasion the old fortifications on the eastern side were demolished and new ones were raised, linking both parts into one urban organism. The lack of space must have forced the inhabitants of Malbork to take down the outer wall. Three gates and a series of triple-walled towers were incorporated into the row of fortifications. The Holy Ghost Gate, also called the Garncarska Gate, led eastwards. Saint Mary's Gate, called the Przewozowa Gate, led southwards, and next to the parish church the Szewska (Shoemakers') Gate led to the north onto the bridge over the Nogat. In addition, there was direct connection of the castle with the town (the pedestrian passage) through the tower and the Furta Gate.

The construction of the planned buildings of the castle-monastery was preceded by preparatory work, mainly earthworks combined with the accumulation of building materials. The hill was shaped appropriately and the moats were carefully dug out to be filled with water flowing down from Lake Dabrowka through a specially built canal.

The construction was begun in 1278 by setting up the circumferential wall in a rectangle measuring 51.5 x 60.7 metres. In the corners of the foundation small towers characteristic of many Teutonic castles were placed. They were raised above the sentry galleries in the final phase of construction and thus accentuated the ornamental peaks of the individual wings and conspicuously fortified the castle with additional defence levels and the possibility of firing into four directions.

The circumferential wall was characterized by a series of architectural devices which made a further interior construction of the rectangle possible and which also had a decisive influence on the location of the castle's entrance. In Malbork the entrance led from the fore-castle (currently the Middle Castle) through the northwest corner. This untypical solution was imposed by the topography of the area.

In the first phase of construction first the north wing, then the south wing were added from the inside. The convent, transferred from Zantyr in 1280, took up residence in the north wing. Here monastery dwellings were prepared as required by the rule. The eastern part, where the chapel of Our Lady was situated on the first floor, was completed at the earliest and was covered with a gable

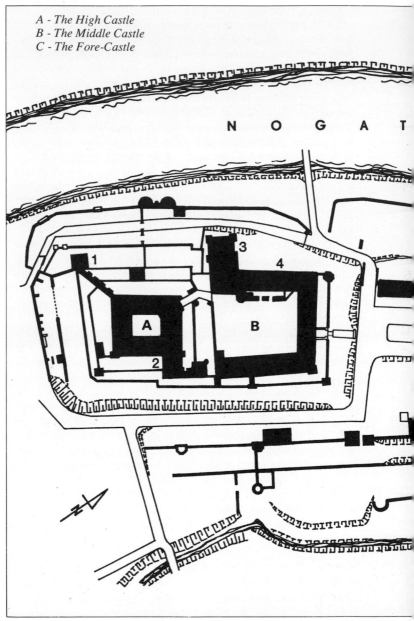

A - *The High Castle*
B - *The Middle Castle*
C - *The Fore-Castle*

N O G A T

Layout of the castle.

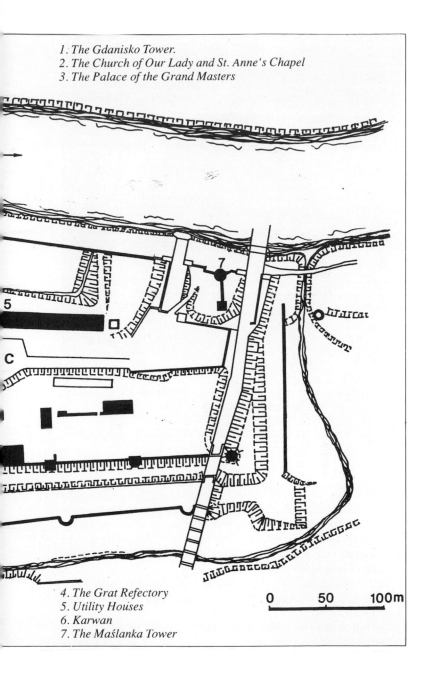

1. *The Gdanisko Tower.*
2. *The Church of Our Lady and St. Anne's Chapel*
3. *The Palace of the Grand Masters*

5

C

7

4. *The Grat Refectory*
5. *Utility Houses*
6. *Karwan*
7. *The Maślanka Tower*

0   50   100m

Portal of the gate leading to the High Castle.

roof. This part, along with the small bell-tower added to the southern facade were the dominating parts of the constructed castle-monastery. On the highest floor, over the chapter-house, temporarily serving as the refectory, was the dormitory. The brothers slept also in one of the ground-floor rooms, probably in the room under the chapel next to the prison cell.

By the end of the 13th century the west wing was built, and in it the refectory, the chamber of the Commander and domestic rooms were located.

The remaining two wings of the rectangle most probably consisted originally of a wooden structure appropriate for stables, workshops and storage facilities.

The church portal »The Golden Gate«.

By the end of the 13th century the convent castle was surrounded by an exterior fortification wall, which also served as a wall of defence encircling the shaped hill. The vast intermural space created as a result of such an architectural scheme served as walking ground, storage premises and as the cemetery of the convent.

At the end of the 13th century two towers were built within the convent castle. The first, called »Klesza« in the 18th century, was situated in the north-eastern corner of the exterior fortification, while the other, »Gdanisko« tower, was raised on the external side of the opposite corner of the castle. The second tower, linked with the fortified monastery by a long covered gallery, served as a tower of ultimate defence and also housed the sanitary facilities.

The Town Hall of Malbork from the second half of the 14th century.

The High Castle from the north-west.

On the northern side (behind the moat) of the castle the fore-castle was situated. It had its own system of defence. For the purpose of creating more room, the surrounding wall (on the northern and western side) was built at the foot of the northern edge of the above-mentioned peninsula, while on the east it was built on a gentle slope. Like the convent castle, it was from the beginning of its creation prepared as a fragment of the future construction. In this way, the construction scheme of the two earliest houses of the fore-castle was laid down. The first house was situated in the south-eastern corner, while the other was raised next to the entrance of the convent castle and housed the armory. Corner turrets were built into the wall, and on the northern side the massive building of the entrance gate was erected. The whole was surrounded by a deep moat with water.

The essential construction program of the convent castle in Malbork was completed in about 1300. The main house of the monastery, from the 16th century called the High Castle, comprised the living quarters of the convent, and the domestic premises were situated at the fore-castle. Further on to the north, in ower areas, building workshops, brickyards and lime kilns were located.

As early as in the first construction phase of the several-storied castle-monastry, many decorative friezes, tracery and above all portals (the Golden Gate) were incorporated and added high artistic and religious values to its modest and austere appearance.

The Refectory of the Convent.

Expansion of the Castle
in the 14th Century

The rise of Malbork Castle, which from 1309 was the seat of the highest dignitary of the Order, was accompanied by a dynamic expansion of the convent house during the whole 14th century and the first half of the 15th century. The typical Commander's castle became the main administrative centre of the Teutonic state and had to meet the requirements of the Grand Master and his court. In the 14th century the still small two-part structure became a triple fortification and was an unconquerable stronghold. The grounds of the former fore-castle were transformed into the second part of the castle, built on the three sides of a trapezoidal courtyard, suitable for representative and administrative functions. All the most important parts of the expanding interior were enlarged: the chapel, the capitular hall, the refectory and the dormitories. A series of new additions, deemed as necessary in governing the states, were also made.

A special architectural design was given to the house erected for the needs of the Grand Master of the Order, called the Palace, built in the form of an impressive residential tower on the western side of the old fore-castle. In the same west wing, next to the Palace, was the Great Refectory – the largest and most splendid interior in the entire secular architecture of the Order. Supported on three slender pillars, the astonishingly spacious vault made this hall monumental in appearance. It was designed for convivial gatherings of the knights – guests from Western Europe, arriving in great numbers to help the Teutonic Knights in their battle against the pagans. The walls of the Great Refectory were at that time covered with a colourful painted decoration representing the Coronation of Our Lady, of which only a small fragment has been preserved to our times. Fourteen large Gothic windows, located in both of the elongated walls, marvelously lighted up this spacious interior, which must have made quite an impression on visitors.

The meals for the tables of the Great Refectory were prepared in the Kitchen, adjoining the north side. The most important element of the Kitchen was the great hearth, covered by a huge chimney hood. Next to the Kitchen was a small room for the cook and a pantry.

The courtyard of the castle.

The Great Refectory in the Middle Castle. Engraving, 18th cent.

In order to serve guests in the basement of the refectory also in the cool months of the year, a two-chamber stove was built for heating the rooms. Altogether there were ten stoves of this type in the castle; they were built for the most important rooms. In the remaining rooms fire-places served a similar purpose. The system of heating the interior with hot air was derived straight from the old heating installation called »hypocaust«.

The number of knights arriving in Malbork from outside of Prussia on their expedition against Lithuania and Samogitia increased over the 14th century. For this reason, the Teutonic Knights built a special residential house on the opposite side of the Middle Castle's courtyard. Apart from the guest chambers, there was also a small chapel devoted to Saint Bartholomew.

The main entrance to the grounds of the Middle Castle remained on the north side. A high gate tower was raised above it, dividing the north wing into two parts. In one of these, on the side of the guest chambers, the apartment and office of the Grand Commander was furnished. In the other part, on the side of the Kitchen and the Great Refectory, there was the castle hospital, called the infirmary. This infirmary, in essence a shelter for the aged and infirm knights, had its own baths, refectory and chapel.

The construction of the second representative part of the castle on the grounds formerly occupied by the fore-castle with its

The Nicholas Gate with the towers of the Bridge Gate.

domestic purpose created the necessity of finding a new place for the domestic facilities. In this way the third, most expansive part of the castle complex came into being, situated north of the Middle Castle. On its eastern side several long houses were situated with one wall adjacent to the main line of the fortification walls. These housed armories, coach-houses and workshops that manufactured spears. On the opposite side, along Nogat River, a huge granary was built, supplied with hoists making it possible to quickly unload boats which carried cargo along the river. In the centre of the newly formed fore-castle there were artisan workshops, stables, barns, fuel storage facilities and also housing for the servants as well as a hospital for the lansquenets. In the middle of the 14th century a church for the servants, called Saint Lawrence, was also built here. At the beginning of the following century, the beautiful figure of Christ praying at Gethsemane was placed in its interior. This unusual work, most probably executed in Toruń workshops, has been preserved till today in the Castle Museum.

Significant constructional changes were also made in the oldest part of the complex, the former convent house, which from the 16th century was called the High Castle. The first castle chapel was enlarged from a small sanctuary located in the compact rectangle of the old castle to the main church of the Teutonic state in Prussia. The structure of the new church protruded significantly

Christ at the Mount of Olives. Sculpture from the 15th cent.

beyond the original rectangle in the eastern direction and was given an interesting architectural setting. The most important element of the exterior decoration was the huge statue of Mary with Child (over 8 metres in height) in the chancel's eastern recess. The figure was made in about 1340 and was richly painted; several decades later it was in addition covered with a colourful mosaic by Venetian artists. The patroness of the Order, looking down from the main castle towards the east, was to have served the role of a guardian over the entire state.

A particularly beautiful setting was given to the new enlarged interior of the church; the one-aisle area, closed from the east, was covered with a star-shaped vault on decorative supports. The lower parts of the supports have the form of figures representing the apostles standing under decorative canopies. Colourful stained glass was mounted in the tall Gothic windows, and the walls were covered with paintings showing figures from the Old and New Testament.

The extension of the church chancel in the eastern direction created a new room under the added part of the construction, i.e. on the ground floor. This was given the function of the sepulchral

Outside view of the Castle Church with the main tower.

chapel of the Grand Masters, devoted to Saint Anne. Two
entrances, located opposite each other in the north and south wall,
led to the chapel interior. Both portals were given a richly sculpted
setting, following the model of the earlier Golden Gate leading to

49

Tympanum at the south portal of Saint Anne's Cahpel.

the church. The figural scenes in the tympana were executed in high relief and covered with colourful paintings: in the north portal there are scenes associated with Saint Mary (The Adoration of the Magi, The Dormition, The Assumption and The Coronation of Our Lady), in the south portal there are Christology scenes (The Ascension, The Last Judgment and the story of finding the Holy Cross). In the crypt underneath the floor the remains of the highest dignitaries of the Order were laid to rest from 1341 onwards. The first to be laid here was Grand Master Dietrich von Altenburg, known for his cruelty but also for his great building activities. In his time, apart from the enlargement of the Church of Our Lady, the construction of the main tower was begun, the Chapel of Saint Anne was completed and the first permanent bridge over Nogat River was built along with the two-towered Bridge Tower to defend it.

Moving the storage facilities to the newly built wing on the east side of the High Tower created new room in the south wing, used for a larger refectory than originally planned. Here a complex of magnificent rooms came into being: the long dining-hall of the convent, covered with the cross-ribbed vault supported on seven pillars, and the after-dinner repose chamber – a high room with a

The courtyard of the High Castle with the Pelican Well.

vault supported on three slender pillars and supplied with a special gallery for musicians.

In the course of the great expansion in the first half of the 14th century, the High Tower acquired its final shape, as it is known from numerous iconographic sources. A rectangular courtyard was created inside by raising a fourth wing on the east side and was surrounded by one-storied galleries. In the centre a deep well was dug out in order to ensure a separate water intake for this part of the stronghold. Stone galleries, providing access to the individual rooms and serving for contemplation, opened on to the courtyard through Gothic windows with rich architectural decoration (tracery) and sculptures (the bases and capitals of the small columns). This courtyard acquired the character of a cloister garth.

Malbork from the south-west. Engraving by Hugo Ulbrich, 1907.

The Teutonic Knights put special emphasis on the defence system of their quarters. As they had built a state of a colonial nature without its own ethnic background, they could not feel safe on Prussian territory. They equipped their head castle with all the defensive elements known in the Middle Ages: moats, towers, curtains, drawbridges, galleries, gate barriers, embrasures, machicolations and hurdles. In the mid-14th century, Malbork Castle was one of the most powerful strongholds in Europe. Its individual parts were surrounded by several rings of massive walls.

In the first half of the 15th century the shape of the castle complex underwent a more significant transformation. After the Battle of Grunwald the Teutonic Knights were no longer able to carry out such extensive construction work as in the 14th century. Owing to the experiences connected with the siege of Malbork by the Polish forces in 1410, they built another fortification line on the eastern and northern side only. The new wall had several semi-cylindrical bastions already adapted for the use of artillery. In its southern part a new entrance gate to the castle was created.

The Grand Master's Palace.

54

Residence of the Grand Masters

After moving the headquarters of the Grand Masters to Malbork in 1309, the necessity of finding suitable dwellings for the supreme dignitary of the Order and his attendants arose. Siegfried von Feuchtwagen most probably resided still at the High Castle, but as early as in the second quarter of the 14th century, the first modest residence was raised in the south-west corner of the old fore-castle. This was a rectangular structure and based on one side on the old fortification wall; adjacent to its side was a small chapel. As conflicts developed within the Order and as the position of the Grand Masters – as the ruling prince-like sovereigns – gradually became stronger, the need for a domicile not of a monastery type but of a courtly and knightly character grew. The conflicts ended with the victory of the concept of the state over the concept of the corporation of monk-knights. In 1382 Grand Master Conrad Zöllner von Rotenstein began to construct a new residence in this spirit. It was raised in the place of the former quadrangular building by 1399. In its architecture the new structure could compete with the finest residences of magnates in Western Europe.

The great western projection, jutting out from the Middle Castle towards the river, took on the shape of a slender residential tower with corners crowned with round turrets. The whole is characterized by splendid proportions and a bold architectural design. The western facade owed its specific lightness and picturesqueness to the large rectangular windows and the rhythm of vertical supports. Behind the windows was the magnificent complex of two representative rooms – the Summer and Winter Refectories, to which the equally magnificent High Vestibule in the Palace's residential section led. The most important element of the architecture of both refectories was their late-Gothic radial vaults supported by one centrally located pillar.

The northern and eastern part of the main floor of the Palace was designed for the private quarters of the Grand Master and his companion, i.e. the dressing-room, the bedroom, the bathroom and other residential rooms. In the neighbourhood of the residential chambers a private chapel, Saint Catherine's, was created for the Grand Masters. It had a chancel projecting a little from the Palace into the courtyard of the Middle Castle. Like the above-mentioned representative rooms, most of these rooms were richly coloured in

The Summer Refectory.

the beginning of the 15th century, which was mainly done in the studio of the court master painter Piotr. The decoration of the vaults usually showed the lush grape-vine or acanthus, while various other motifs, such as ornamental or sometimes heraldic figures, appeared on the walls. A frequently used element was the painted imitation of hanging curtains.

The Long Corridor. Water-Colour by J. C. Schultz, 19th century.

The south facade of the Palace.

There was an interesting group of paintings in the Winter Refectory. Here was the gallery of the Grand Masters of the Order, similar to the older gallery, in the first half of the 14th century executed on the eastern and southern wall of the capitular hall in the High Castle. Unfortunately, only small fragments of the Palace's rich painting decoration have survived till today. They have been carefully preserved and exhibited. A better preserved exception is the restored painting in the Low Vestibule: the grape-vine on the vault and the coat of arms of Grand Master Conrad von Jungingen over the entrance to the residential quarters as well as the paintings in the chamber next to Saint Catherine's Chapel and the beautiful figures of the four holy virgins on the northern wall of the bedroom: Saint Margaret, Saint Dorothy, Saint Catherine and Saint Barbara.

All of the most important rooms were on the first floor (above ground level) and served the Teutonic Knights as the main floor. On the ground floor, which had a separate entrance from the courtyard, there were the Order's archives and chancellery, run by writers. It is possible that here was also the small chancellery, i.e. the personal chancellery of the Grand Master himself, which started its work in the second quarter of the 14th century, in the time when Werner von Orseln was in charge of the corporation.

The individual elements of the Palace show influences of Western European architecture, particularly English and Burgundian. However, as a whole it is a wonderful creation of human genius, a jewel of medieval architecture, not inferior to the best works of the time.

Illustrissimus et Excellentissimus Dñus Geerhardus Comes
à Döenhoff, Palatinus Pomerelliæ, Terrarum Prussiæ
Thesaurarius Capt : Mariæburgens : SKarzeviens :
Bernens : Luciniens : Felinens : Regiæ Oeconomiæ
Mariæburgensis Administrator. etc

Guilielmus Hondius Hago Batavos ad vivum Delniavit et æri insidit.
1643.

Wilhelm Hondius. Engraving by Gerhard Denhoff, 1643.

The Period of Polish Rule

The sharp conflict between the autocratic Teutonic rule and its subjects, which was increasing over the first half of the 15th century, led to the outbreak of an anti-Teutonic rising in Prussia at the beginning of 1454. At the same time, a deputation of the Prussian states, headed by Jan Bażyński, asked the Polish king for help. Kazimierz Jagiellończyk drew up an incorporation act, which incorporated the Prussian lands into the Polish Crown. This led to the long Thirteen Years' War between Poland and the Order, which ended with the signing of the Peace of Toruń in 1466. The peace contract was Poland's success because it regained Gdańsk Pomerania, the district of Chełmno and took over from the Teutonic Order Żuławy, part of Warmia and Pomesania; these lands were joined together and built the province Royal Prussia. As early as in 1457, Malbork Castle was taken over by Poles who bought it from the mercenary troops stationed there, because Grand Master Ludwig von Erlichshausen was unable to pay their dues. From this time the fate of Malbork was closely bound with the history of the Polish state and nation, while the capital of the Teutonic state was moved to Królewiec (Kaliningrad, Königsberg).

Malbork became the seat of high offices of the Polish administration: the starost, or head of a district, who was each time appointed by the king and the voivod, and from the beginning of the 16th century also the steward and treasurer of the Prussian lands. The castle, once the capital centre and seat of state authority, was for the Republic one of the many fortified points at the periphery of the country. However, its significance as a stronghold and supply base in the case of war was acknowledged. The burgrave cared for the maintenance and furnishing of the castle and was appointed especially for this purpose by the starost.

A considerable quantity of war equipment, stored mainly in the old armory at the fore-castle, proves that Malbork at that time served as one of the biggest arsenals of the Republic. Among those who appreciated its role was King Stefan Batory, who in 1577 organized his base of attack here during the fighting with the rebelling city of Gdańsk. Two hundred military men were assigned to the castle for good; this number could of course be increased in case of emergency.

East wing of the middle Castle.

During the first one and a half centuries of Polish rule, few changes were brought about in the Gothic appearance of the castle. There was no need for this at any rate. The Middle Castle retained its former residential-administrative function. In the old Palace of the Grand Masters one of the residences of Polish kings was established in order to be used by monarchs during their visits to Prussia. In the north and east wing officials lived who represented royal as well as local authority: the starost, the treasurer, the steward and the burgrave. Here they also had their offices. Like the Middle Castle, most of the houses at the fore-castle retained their former function. Only the High Castle was now mainly used as a large domestic place (food storage), and some premises were occupied by commanders of the castle forces. The Church of Our Lady became a branch of the town's parish church.

In the second half of the 16th century the Treasurer Jan Kostka built a wooden residential mansion on the southern edge of the Middle Castle courtyard; conditions in the cold and damp brick interior must have been very hard, at any rate the house constituted a kind of fourth wing of this part of the stronghold. In the 1580s the subsequent Treasurer, Jan Dulski, built a Renaissance dome on the main tower, which had been crenelated until then. The bell was also hung in the tower then with large clock faces on the outside walls.

Entrance to the north wing of the Middle Castle.

The Palace of the royal residence was furnished in the 15th and 16th centuries without introducing any changes. King Kazimierz Jagiellończyk as well as Aleksander or Stefan Batory later stayed in the old apartments of the Grand Master when they were in Malbork. Later, in about 1600, Zygmunt III Waza had the eastern part of the church rebuilt into a representative staircase, and from the room adjacent to the chapel a new passage was built, leading diagonally to the Winter Refectory. The interior of the Refectory itself was divided by a wooden ceiling into two storeys, which were also given partition walls. The new royal rooms were furnished with tile stoves and contemporary installations.

In 1626 Malbork met with another terrible war disaster. The castle was taken by the hostile Swedish forces. In the course of the fight, the artillery damaged and even completely devastated some buildings at the fore-castle and many parts of the roofs of the High and Middle Castle. Shortly after the war was over and Malbork had been returned to Poland (1635), the great fire of 1644 multiplied the losses by destroying first of all the roofs of the High Castle, the Gdanisko Tower and the Renaissance dome on the main tower. The energetic starost Gerhard Denhoff needed but a few years to rebuild most of the ruined parts. The grand-scale repairs of roofs and walls, the renovation of devastated rooms and their new furnishing were interrupted by the second Polish-Swedish war of

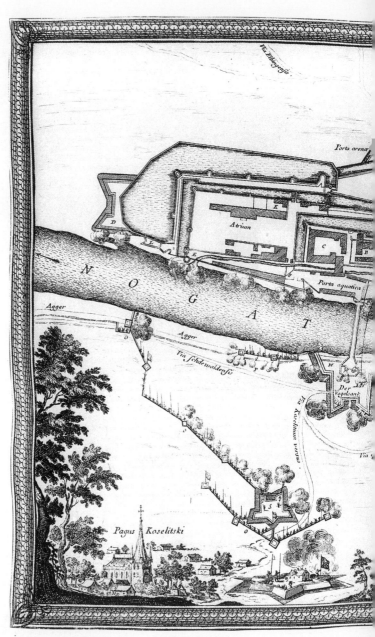

Layout of the Castle. Engraving from 1659.

Porta figlina

Via versus Graudensium et Thorunium

Porta Merckenia.

Forum

F L U V I U S

Agger

Ionanum

Ichnographia
Oppidi et Castri MARIEBURGI in Prussia Re
gali, a foederatis Austriacorum, et Polonorum Exercitibus, d. 12 Julij An:
1659. obsidione cincti, sed quæ 30. Septemb. eiusdem anni iterum solvebatur.
Notarum Explicatio.
A. Oppid. Marieburgum. B. Castrum Vetus. C. Castrum Novum. D. Opera à Suecis
nuper exstata. E. Turris Buttermilchs Turm dicta. F Turris Räketurni. G. Turris Civin
H. Turris Dantiscanorum. I. Pistrinum. K. Armamentarium. L. Forcipulæ vulgo Te:
nadle. M. Mortaria Suecorum. N. Mortaria Polonorum. O. Polon. Opera et acces:
sus P Suecor. access. quib? hosti obviam ibatur. Q. Suggest. Polon. octo maiorib?.
et duob? minorib. tormentis instructus. R. Dolium pilis Granatensib? repletum a
Polon. aggeri infossü. S. Castella.Polon. Campestre. T. Templ. Marieburgense.
Scala 30. Pert. Rhinl. 30.

65

The Palace from the south.

1655-1660, known as the »deluge«. With it the gradual decline of the military significance of Malbork began. In the royal treasury there were no resources left for maintaining the stronghold. In addition, various armies fighting in the Northern War (1700-1721), such as Russian, Saxon, Swedish and others, passed through.

More significant building activity was then shown only by the Jesuits, who had been residing in several dwellings of the High Castle already since 1618. In the second half of the 17th century they put in order and renovated the interior of the castle church and also financed the baroque furnishings of the church; apart from the four altars and the pulpit, they purchased the organ body and benches. As the hitherto occupied seat was not sufficient for the Jesuits, in about the middle of the 18th century they built a several-storied college building near the castle church. This building survived a little more than a hundred years until the restoration of the castle at the end of the 19th century.

Owing to the gradual decline of the castle's military significance, visible at the end of the 17th and throughout the 18th century, its exterior fortifications slowly went to ruin. The walls of

Coat of arms of King Zygmunt III Wasa in the Palace.

the fore-castle were used by the builders of the new houses, which at that time were more and more built around the High Castle and the Middle Castle. Directly after the middle of the 18th century, the starost Michal Ernest Rexin made a worthwile attempt to restore its old function to the stronghold by renovating the premises used by officials at the Middle Castle, repairing the roofs of the High Castle and raising a new impressive baroque dome on the main tower.

In the more than three centuries of Polish rule, certain changes in the Gothic appearance of the castle and in the form of its interior architecture were brought about; these ensued from the adjustments to the current needs of the occupants as well as from the manner of carrying out repairs after the numerous devastations. However, the structure retained its original form without any significant transformations until the 1770s. This was possible thanks to the presence of a permanent occupant during all this time, who had a specific view as to how the castle was to be used. This to a certain degree was a continuation of its original functions.

Portcullis at the gateway of the Middle Castle.

68

The Military Significance of Malbork

The strategic significance of each historical stronghold first of all depended on its place in the defence system and on its location as regards the natural defence conditions. Sometimes other factors were also decisive, for example political or economic. The significance of fortifications underwent frequent changes in the course of history, as can be shown by the example of Malbork.

The construction of the castle in Malbork was first of all determined by the necessity of making the strategic points along the western border of the Teutonic state, which was in the process of organizing itself, more dense. On the lands from Toruń all the way up to the Sambian Peninsula they were loosely scattered. From the second half of the 13th century the Order had only one stronghold in Zantyr, between Kwidzyń and Elbląg. The lowland location of this place, in the valley of the Vistula, was regarded as unfavourable, even though it was an excellent point of controlling navigation in the direction of Gdansk as well as of Elbląg. The region of the fork of the Vistula and Nogat Rivers had been a strategic point for Pomerania since the early Middle Ages. Its military role increased in the Middle Ages and in modern times. Why then, was it not decided to expand Zantyr or to transfer it to the upland into the nearest vicinity of the Mątowski Headland? Instead, it was decided to build another new stronghold in a place about 20 km up north. Such a decision was no doubt the result of several factors: 1. the strategic point in Zantyr remained under the rule of the Order; 2. a new seat of the convent was built, which when raised in a more convenient place (well projected into Żuławy) made military and economic control of the fertile Vistula and Nogat delta possible for the following years; 3. the construction of the castle in Malbork had a political-military aspect, which is indicated first by the possession of the Gniewa district, then of the whole of Pomerania. These events, together with the construction of the castle in Malbork, took place simultaneously and formed part of the general policy of the Order and a gauge of its economic and military strength.

From the beginning of the construction of the castle in Malbork, the Order put great emphasis on the expansion of the defence system. This was particularly visible after the seat of the supreme authority had been transferred from Venice to Malbork in 1309.

The convent house was transformed into the capital seat of the Teutonic state. The rank was higher and accordingly, the Malbork stronghold was expanded .

From the beginning of the 15th century, on an area of about 21 hectares (about 52 acres), a triple fortification structure was built linking monastery functions (the High Castle) with economic functions (the Low Castle). This was emphasized by the numerous fortification wall lines, moats with water and other elements of the defence system (sentry galleries, embrasures, machicolations, gratings, gates, towers…). The greatest concentration of these was within the High Castle. This part of the stronghold, the highest storied, dominated over the whole, emphasizing the leading military role synchronized with the monastery function. The combination of these two functions illustrated the organizational essence of the Order.

The whole of the castle was arranged in accordance with its surroundings along the high edge of the Nogat and covered an area of over 800 m. The width of the fortifications did not exceed 250 m. In 1365 the castle was merged with the city walls and thus extended Malbork's defence system by a further 450 m.

The narrow and at the same time long fortification structure had not been adapted to military defence until the beginning of the 15th century. It can be assumed that in Malbork the belief in the power of the Order was strong and until 1410 the possibility of a direct attack on the main castle had not been taken into account.

The unsuccessful Polish siege (particularly the cannon firing together with the crushing defeat at Grunwald) was a shock for the defenders of Malbork. Conclusions were immediately drawn from this lesson in strategy, and the construction of a defence system was begun on the eastern foreground of the castle, in the course of time adapting it to the use of fire-arms. During the Thirteen Years' War these seemed to be sufficiently strong because the attacks of Polish forces were repelled many times.

About 40 years before the siege of Malbork, Teutonic castles were equipped with fire-arms, for example in 1374 the castle in Lipiennik was armed with three cannons. In Malbork cannons were manufactured at the Low Castle from the beginning of the 15th century. In the years 1401-1409 at least 24 gun-barrels were cast in the Malbork foundry, of which in the words of Jan of Żuławka, a Teutonic chronicler, one was a large bombard incomparable to any other in the country. Gun-carriages, stone and lead gun shells were also manufactured here. The latter were for the small »cans«, i.e. for harquebuses.

Draw-bridge over the moat at the High Castle.

The south wing of the High Castle.

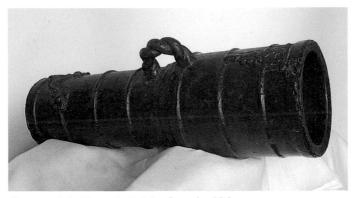

Cannon of the Teutonic Knights from the 15th century.

The inevitably approaching armed conflict with Poland forced the Order to intensify its production of arms. In the years 1401-1403, 60 »grzywnas« were spent on fire-arms, and five years later twenty times as much.

It cannot be ruled out that the oldest Teutonic bombard with an image of the Virgin Mary, found at the castle in Kurzętnik in 1941, comes from Malbork. Other centrcs, such as Gdańsk for example, had a much smaller production.

The quickly accelerating production proves that the Order recognized the advantages of fire-arms. All innovations as regards war techniques were conveyed not only by paid craftsmen, but also by members of the Teutonic Order. In the years 1408-1409 the main foundry of the Order in Malbork was directed by brother Jahan, who was a specialist molder, most probably trained in Western Europe. The situation was similar as to the production of other types of weapons. The military resources in the main castle were not only the most numerous, but also the most modern. Other »komturias« which had no specialized workshops were also furnished from the Malbork arsenal. Mercenary troops which served in columns, infantry and which also constituted a part of the castle forces were mostly armed with these weapons.

The Order's arms resources were used by the guests who came to Malbork – the knights who were to take part in the »Prussian journeys«. The castle in Malbork was the chief meeting place. Before the expeditions magnificent feasts, tournaments and hunts were held here. The most valiant knights were awarded with costly gifts and also often with the knight's belt.

The south-east corner of the High Castle.

The richness of the feasts, the magnificence and hugeness of the castle's architecture are only some of the forms of psychological influence and winning the Western knighthood over. However, when there was war between Poland and Lithuania, the Teutonic Knights had the assistance of knights mostly from the German-speaking countries, who gathered under the sign of Saint George.

The reserves of all types of arms in the central arsenal radically decreased after the Grunwald defeat. However, unsettled war strifes led again to the production of arms. As early as until 1448, the arms supply had been considerably rebuilt. However, the quantitative proportion changed in favour of fire-arms. The subsequent years, characterized by the actions of the Thirteen Years' War, confirmed the correctness of this trend and the necessity of building a new type of shielding fortifications in front of the Malbork stronghold.

After the second Peace at Torun (1466), the castle in Malbork lost its leading position in the Teutonic state and became the centre (administrative, economic and especially military) of the newly formed Polish district – Royal Prussia. This made it necessary to maintain the castle in an appropriate state of defence. This moment was recognized by all the (frequently changing) rulers of Malbork and the defence system was accordingly expanded.

The development of modern defence fortifications in Malbork dates back to the work carried out on the initiative of the Polish Treasurer Jan Dulski at the end of the 16th century. At that time no new defence elements were built. Instead, the medieval walls were adapted for the defense with fire-arms.

The new fortifications of the old-Dutch type are ascribed to the Swedes. They were most probably made directly after the first taking over of the castle in 1626. Further fortification work was carried out in the years of the »Swedish deluge« (1656-1660) and before and during the Northern War (1700-1721). The last modern fortifications of Malbork together with the entrenchments on the western side within the village Kałdowo were constructed during the Napoleonic campaign.

With the development of fire-arms, the castle slowly lost its strategic meaning. However, at the end of the 18th and at the beginning of the 19th century it continued to serve military purposes as barracks, field hospital and storage facilities. The conservation work begun in 1817 ended the castle's military career, or it rather seemed so at that time. Unfortunately, in the final phase of the Second World War, the castle and town were once more transformed into a fortress.

The toilet tower of the infirmary.

The Castle Church from the east, drawing by F. Gilly, 1799.

Under Prussian Rule

In 1772 the forces of Frederick the Great entered Malbork by virtue of the treaty on the partition of Poland, concluded between Prussia, Russia and Austria. This signified the beginning of one of the most dramatic periods in the history of the fortress. The devastations that occurred were the result of economic difficulties as well as the limited practicality of the Prussian administration, and also of the then negative German attitude to the traditions of the Teutonic Order and the low esteem for its architecture. The reconstruction of the castle into military barracks (1773-1774), and somewhat later the reconstruction into a military storage place (1801-1804) caused irreversible damage. A »victim« of the wide-scale dismantling was the entire old interior construction of three wings of the High Castle and two wings of the Middle Castle. The vaults were demolished, new rectangular windows were forced in and a part of the towers at the fore-castle was taken down. The changing of the Palace interior into weaving workshops and dwellings for the workers (1785-1786) was combined with the introduction of a two-level structure in the formerly representative interior and the demolition of the vaults of the smaller rooms next to the Winter Refectory as well as the breaking down of the stone window crosses in both refectories. In the Great Refectory a square for military drill was built, which led to the devastation of the decoration and furnishing of this splendid room. In addition, at the end of the 18th century the government Councillor David Gilly put forward the project for demolishing the entire castle in order to obtain material for building new storage houses.

At the same time, in the milieu of the young German romantics, a movement arose towards the recognition of Malbork as a »valuable monument of old building methods«. In 1799 an album with a series of graphic views of the castle was issued, drawn in aquatint by Friedrich Frick, mainly on the basis of the drawings of Friedrich Gilly. These pictures, which were outstanding from the artistic and technical point of view, played a great role in awakening the consciousness of the German society, mainly of circles in Berlin, who stood up against a further devastation of the historical structures. In 1804 a government order was given by King Frederick William III commanding that the castle should be handled with appropriate care.

The commencement of the then planned restoration work was interrupted by the Napoleonic wars for ten years or more; the brief sojourn of French forces at the castle (1807) multiplied its damages all the more. It was only in 1817 that the planned work of recreating the structures from the times of its greatest splendour was undertaken. Up to the middle of the last century, this first, in writings called »romantic« restoration was carried out under the spiritual patronage of the leading president of Prussia, Theodor von Schön, who wanted to make the castle a holy place of the highest significance for the whole province. The construction work was headed by the engineer Carl August Gersdorff during most of this period, and official supervision was entrusted to the German architect Karl Friedrich Schinkel.

The High Castle continued to serve as a military storage place, the romantic restoration included only the Middle Castle, mainly the Palace of the Grand Masters. Considerable funds from the State Treasury, which were obtained thanks to the endeavours of von Schön, made it possible to carry out the work quickly. As early as towards the end of the 1820s, the representative interior of the Palace, deprived of the secondary divisions, regained its old appearance. Then, on the request of Schinkel, the exterior walls of the west and north wing were crowned with a crenelle. This was a result of a wrong impression of Gothic architecture, like the high triangular peak raised over the Grand »Komturia« seat in the north wing at the end of the romantic reconstruction. Today it would be futile to look for those elements characteristic of the Gothic style at that time; we only know them from the archival photographs and the old views of the castle. Subsequent generations of conservators from the 19th century regarded these elements as historically unjustified and therefore they were dismantled.

In the middle of the last century the scientific conservation of monuments developed and was in practice begun by the known French architect Eugene Emmanuel Viollet-le-Duc. The national protection of historical monuments was given an official framework. In 1843 the Office of Monument Conservation was set up in Pomerania, and Ferdinand von Quast was appointed for this post. In his important work on Malbork Castle (1851) he not only criticized the effects of its romantic restoration, but also was the first to give a chronology of the construction of Malbork that was close to our present knowledge. F. von Quast launched the scientific approach to the conservation of the castle based on reliable knowledge of its architecture. He himself also carried out the first surveys and studies on the grounds of the High Castle. Von

The north wing of the Middle Castle. Engraving by Rosenheyn, 1858.

Quast's concept was fully realized by Konrad Steinbrecht at the end of the century.

In the 1870s two anniversaries drew the attention of the authorities to the Teutonic fortress: the one hundredth anniversary of merging the Malbork district with the kingdom of Prussia (1872) and the six hundredth anniversary of the town of Malbork (1876), celebrated in the presence of Emperor William I and the heir to the throne. The decision on its construction was made in 1877, and the young architect Conrad Steinbrecht was entrusted with the work.

The principles of the romantic restoration in the first half of the 19th century, in accordance with which it was not necessary to faithfully imitate the past, were an obvious contrast to the program of the scientific reconstruction of the castle in the spirit of purity of style, which began in 1882 and caused its second reconstruction. It was carried out in compliance with the architectural data and the results of the archival studies and excavation research. In the beginning, all the elements from periods later than the Middle

The High Castle after its restoration by Konrad Steinbrecht.

Konrad Steinbrecht (1849-1923).

Ages were removed. Then all architectural elements were taken from the rubble and the excavations and were then segregated and compared with the details preserved »in situ«. After analyzing the results of the studies, an attempt at graphically recreating the original appearance of each part of a structure was made. After the design had been approved by competent authorities in Gdańsk and Berlin, the work was taken up. The reconstruction of missing fragments and details was executed on the basis of models of other Teutonic castles as well as of fortresses and monasteries of Western Europe.

An undertaking planned on such a large scale required considerable financial outlays. As in the case of the reconstruction of the cathedral in Cologne, the money was mainly gathered through a lottery run by a public society for the reconstruction of the castle in Malbork.

The High Castle, photograph from 1885.

Steinbrecht devoted nearly all of his professional life to the reconstruction of Malbork. The effect of his work was the restoration of the castle to an appearance that was close to that it could have had in the times of the Order's splendour. Thanks to the detailed reconstruction of the whole system of defence elements and installations, the reconstructed fortress became an example of the development of medieval fortifications. In order to complete the work the reconstructor provided the interior with more or less successful copies of the medieval furnishings; this was to create an illusion of the life in the castle, as if the monk-knights had just left their headquarters.

At the beginning of the 1890s, the castle was prepared as one of the residences of the emperor of Germany; the emperor's apartments were established in the old Palace of the Grand Masters. Gradually, more or less from the times of the First World War, the complex took on the functions of a museum, although until the times of the Second World War an institution called »museum« did not exist in the castle.

After the death of Steinbrecht in 1923, the work in Malbork was headed by his friend and successor, the known conservator of Prussia, Bernhard Schmid. He was mainly engaged in the reconstruction of the exterior fortifications of the castle's eastern and western side.

Coloured window in the staircase.

The Castle after 1945

The disaster of the Second World War did not spare Malbork Castle. Changed into a fortress by the Nazis towards the end of the war, it defended itself against the attacks of the Soviet forces for nearly two months. The result of these fights was the almost complete destruction of the eastern facade of the High and Middle Castle – the main tower came down, the peak over the chamber of the convent fell, the chapel of Saint Anne and the church above it were blown up, the southern part of the eastern wing at the Middle Castle ceased to exist. The gun fire also tore apart the interior of the Clerical Tower, the Bell-Ringer House and the eastern facade of the Palace of the Grand Masters including a fragment of the vault in the corner room. The intensive fire of the fore-castle shattered nearly all of the houses in this part of the castle. Great heaps of rubble, glass, broken furniture and doors were scattered about in the courtyards, the moats and the interiors. Torn roofs, stripped walls and torn out doors brought in snow and frost as well as rain and dust. The degree of the devastation of the historical complex in 1945 is estimated at about 50%.

Today only archival photographs document the picture of those tragic days. It is already for the third time that scrupulous conservators, this time of Polish origin, through painstaking work restored the castle nearly to its original splendour.

During the first five years after the war, the ruined fortress remained under the management of the Museum of the Polish Army in Warsaw. There were plans for opening a branch of the museum here. For this reason the first measures were taken to clean up and safeguard the fortress. The castle grounds were cleared of mines and the gates were repaired. A very important step was to repair a large part of the damaged roofs, which protected the historical structure against the destructive influence of the atmosphere until the time of the planned reconstruction. Over the next ten years, the castle was under the care of the Polish Tourist Country-Lovers' Association (PTTK). Incessantly growing tourism led to other necessary restoration measures. However, these were of a provisional nature and were carried out without detailed documentation. Towards the end of the 1950s the Social Committee for the Reconstruction of the Castle, founded by local culture activists, became the initiator of actions towards the

Malbork in ruins after the Second World War.

protection and the cleaning up of the complex. The work was accelerated, and in addition the Committee took up endeavours to establish a museum institution in the castle.

The decision on the further fate of the post-Teutonic fortress was accelerated by the fire that burnt down the roofs of the western and northern wing of the Middle Castle on the night between September 7th and 8th 1959. It became a kind of turning point in the post-war history of the complex and led up to the appointment of a suitable custodian of the castle. From January 1st 1961 the castle's management was in the hands of the newly created Castle Museum, established primarily for the purpose of reconstructing, conservating and maintaining the castle complex.

In the first stage of the restoration tasks, which was completed at the beginning of the 1970s, the exterior structures of the High and Middle Castle were merged into the shape known from the oldest iconographic sources. The interiors of these two parts of the complex were adapted to the purpose of exhibiting and storing the works of art as well as of administering the museum. The view of the castle on the side facing the town was also put in order by restoring the damaged walls of defence on the eastern and southern side. At the beginning of the 1980s, the second stage of reconstruction began, consisting in the gradual restoration and development of the most valuable structures of the fore-castle and the conservation of the old interior decoration of the High and Middle Castle.

Conservation and maintaining the historical complex is now the most important task of the young Malbork museum. This is a museum with various departments, such as historical and artistic ones. It is mainly devoted to matters of reconstruction, management and proper maintenance of the castle. Parallel to these tasks, the museum is also leading the scientific research into the castle's architecture and history, into the primeval history of the Lower Powiśle and the history and artistic culture of Royal Prussia. Further tasks of the Malbork post are typical museum jobs, such as gathering, securing and studying the works of old and contemporary art as well as presenting them to the public. On the threshold of its activity the museum had only those objects of the old collection at its disposal that had survived the war damages and the wave of plunders from the years 1945-1946. Apart from the collection of architectural elements, there were a few examples of medieval sculpture and pseudo-Gothic furniture from the turn of the 19th and 20th centuries. Today the Malbork collection comprises the collection of medieval architectural details regarded

The tombstone-plate of Ostrowin, Castle Museum Malbork.

Exhibits from the Castle Museum. Top left: monstrance of Otto Schwerdfeger. Bottom left: amber casket from the late 17th century.

as the largest in Europe, the collection of works of art made of amber – unique on a world scale –, an impressive collection of old side and fire-arms, and a rich collection of coins and medals that goes back to the historical mints of Malbork. The various objects of interest collected after 1961 are supplemented by the collection

Above: altar of the chapel in Tenkitten from 1504.

of Gothic sculpture, old china and building ceramics, Polish china
from workshops in Korzec and Baranówka, faience, products of
old artistic smithery and foundry as well as collections of
drawings, furniture, paintings, stained glass, artistic glass and
finally an impressive collection of contemporary ex libris

93

General view of the castle.

inscriptions. As a result of many years of archaeological studies, abundant material has been collected that illustrates the ancient history of the lands situated east of the lower course of Vistula River. For more than a decade now, the open-air event called »Sound and Light« has been taking place in the picturesque scenery of the castle courtyards. At present this is the only event of this type in Poland and its scenario is based on selected episodes

from the stormy history of Malbork. At dusk, thanks to modern technology, a meeting with the castle and its history takes place, leaving unforgettable impressions.

Today Malbork Castle is one of the greatest tourist attractions in Poland. The largest brick fortress of medieval Europe continues to fascinate because of its greatness, its beautiful architecture, its bold construction and fine detail.

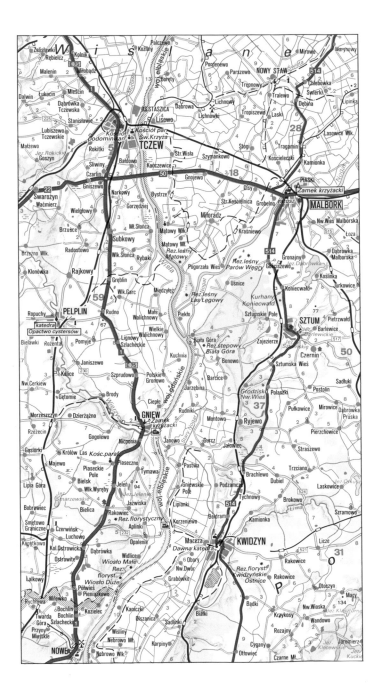